Breathing Is Racist

-Check Your Privilege, Mother Nature-

By Albert Huston

Albert Huston

Table of Contents:

Breathing Is Racist

Albert Huston

"Politics is not a game, but a serious business."

\-   Winston Churchill

Breathing Is Racist

Albert Huston

Just kidding, that's silly.

Breathing Is Racist

Just kidding, that's silly.

Albert Huston

Just kidding, that's silly.

Breathing Is Racist

Just kidding, that's silly.

Albert Huston

Just kidding, that's silly.

Just kidding, that's silly.

Albert Huston

Just kidding, that's silly.

Just kidding, that's silly.

Albert Huston

Just kidding, that's silly.

Just kidding, that's silly.

Albert Huston

Just kidding, that's silly.

Just kidding, that's silly.

Albert Huston

Just kidding, that's silly.

Just kidding, that's silly.

Albert Huston

Just kidding, that's silly.

Just kidding, that's silly.

Albert Huston

Just kidding, that's silly.

Breathing Is Racist

Just kidding, that's silly.

Albert Huston

Just kidding, that's silly.

Just kidding, that's silly.

Albert Huston

Just kidding, that's silly.

Just kidding, that's silly.

Albert Huston

Just kidding, that's silly.

Just kidding, that's silly.

Albert Huston

Just kidding, that's silly.

Just kidding, that's silly.

Albert Huston

Just kidding, that's silly.

Breathing Is Racist

Just kidding, that's silly.

Albert Huston

Just kidding, that's silly.

Just kidding, that's silly.

Albert Huston

Just kidding, that's silly.

Breathing Is Racist

Just kidding, that's silly.

Albert Huston

Just kidding, that's silly.

Just kidding, that's silly.

Albert Huston

Just kidding, that's silly.

Breathing Is Racist

Just kidding, that's silly.

Albert Huston

Just kidding, that's silly.

Just kidding, that's silly.

Albert Huston

Just kidding, that's silly.

Just kidding, that's silly.

Albert Huston

Just kidding, that's silly.

Just kidding, that's silly.

Albert Huston

Just kidding, that's silly.

Just kidding, that's silly.

Albert Huston

Just kidding, that's silly.

Just kidding, that's silly.

Albert Huston

Just kidding, that's silly.

Just kidding, that's silly.

Albert Huston

Just kidding, that's silly.

Just kidding, that's silly.

Albert Huston

Just kidding, that's silly.

Just kidding, that's silly.

Albert Huston

Just kidding, that's silly.

Just kidding, that's silly.

Albert Huston

Just kidding, that's silly.

Breathing Is Racist

Just kidding, that's silly.

Albert Huston

Just kidding, that's silly.

Just kidding, that's silly.

Albert Huston

Just kidding, that's silly.

Just kidding, that's silly.

Albert Huston

Just kidding, that's silly.

Breathing Is Racist

Just kidding, that's silly.

Albert Huston

Just kidding, that's silly.

Breathing Is Racist

Just kidding, that's silly.

Albert Huston

Just kidding, that's silly.

Just kidding, that's silly.

Albert Huston

Just kidding, that's silly.

Just kidding, that's silly.

Albert Huston

Just kidding, that's silly.

Breathing Is Racist

Just kidding, that's silly.

Albert Huston

Just kidding, that's silly.

Just kidding, that's silly.

Albert Huston

Just kidding, that's silly.

Just kidding, that's silly.

Albert Huston

Just kidding, that's silly.

Just kidding, that's silly.

Albert Huston

Just kidding, that's silly.

Just kidding, that's silly.

Albert Huston

Just kidding, that's silly.

Just kidding, that's silly.

Albert Huston

Just kidding, that's silly.

Just kidding, that's silly.

Albert Huston

Just kidding, that's silly.

Breathing Is Racist

Just kidding, that's silly.

Albert Huston

Just kidding, that's silly.

Just kidding, that's silly.

Albert Huston

Just kidding, that's silly.

Just kidding, that's silly.

Albert Huston

Just kidding, that's silly.

Breathing Is Racist

Just kidding, that's silly.

Albert Huston

Just kidding, that's silly.

Just kidding, that's silly.

Albert Huston

Just kidding, that's silly.

Just kidding, that's silly.

Albert Huston

Just kidding, that's silly.

Just kidding, that's silly.

Albert Huston

Just kidding, that's silly.

Breathing Is Racist

Just kidding, that's silly.

Albert Huston

Just kidding, that's silly.

Just kidding, that's silly.

Albert Huston

Just kidding, that's silly.

Just kidding, that's silly.

Albert Huston

Just kidding, that's silly.

Just kidding, that's silly.

Albert Huston

Just kidding, that's silly.

Just kidding, that's silly.

Albert Huston

Just kidding, that's silly.

Just kidding, that's silly.

Albert Huston

Just kidding, that's silly.

Breathing Is Racist

Just kidding, that's silly.

Albert Huston

Just kidding, that's silly.

Breathing Is Racist

Just kidding, that's silly.

Albert Huston

Just kidding, that's silly.

Just kidding, that's silly.

Albert Huston

Just kidding, that's silly.

Just kidding, that's silly.

Albert Huston

Just kidding, that's silly.

Just kidding, that's silly.

Albert Huston

Just kidding, that's silly.

Just kidding, that's silly.

Albert Huston

Just kidding, that's silly.

Just kidding, that's silly.

Albert Huston

Just kidding, that's silly.

Just kidding, that's silly.

Albert Huston

Just kidding, that's silly.

Just kidding, that's silly.

Albert Huston

Just kidding, that's silly.

Just kidding, that's silly.

Albert Huston

Just kidding, that's silly.

Breathing Is Racist

Just kidding, that's silly.

Albert Huston

Just kidding, that's silly.

Breathing Is Racist

Just kidding, that's silly.

Albert Huston

Just kidding, that's silly.

Breathing Is Racist

Just kidding, that's silly.

Albert Huston

Just kidding, that's silly.

Just kidding, that's silly.

Albert Huston

Just kidding, that's silly.

Just kidding, that's silly.

Albert Huston

Just kidding, that's silly.

Just kidding, that's silly.

Albert Huston

Just kidding, that's silly.

Just kidding, that's silly.

Albert Huston

Just kidding, that's silly.

Just kidding, that's silly.

Albert Huston

Just kidding, that's silly.

Just kidding, that's silly.

Albert Huston

Just kidding, that's silly.

Breathing Is Racist

www.ingramcontent.com/pod-product-compliance
Lightning Source LLC
Chambersburg PA
CBHW051306250726
48656CB00004B/1509